STRUCTURES

Malcolm Dixon

Illustrations by Jenny Hughes

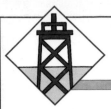

Exploring Technology

Bridges and Tunnels
Communications
Flight
Land Transport
Machines
Structures
Textiles
Water Transport

Cover: *The Oakland Bridge, San Francisco, USA, with skyscrapers in the background.*

For Michelle and Joanne

Series Editor: Sue Hadden
Book Editor: Joan Walters
Designer: Malcolm Walker, Kudos Designs

First published in 1990 by
Wayland (Publishers) Ltd
61 Western Road, Hove
East Sussex BN3 1JD, England

British Library Cataloguing in Publication Data
Dixon, Malcolm *1946–*
    Structures.
    1. Structures
    I. Title II. Hughes, Jenny III. Series
    624

    ISBN 1 85210 932 7

Phototypeset by Nicola Taylor, Wayland.
Printed in Turin, Italy by G. Canale & C.S.p.A
Bound in France by A.G.M.

CONTENTS

Reshaping our world

We are surrounded by interesting structures created by humans and by nature. The natural structures, such as rocks and those in the animal and plant worlds, have developed over millions of years. Human-made structures show how people have attempted to control their environment. Early men and women used simple tools and natural materials to build shelters. Over hundreds of years new materials, skills and powerful machinery have been developed to help build structures of all shapes and sizes, and for many different purposes.

Designers and builders have had to overcome many problems. They have had to plan their work carefully

A part of Australia's coastline forms a magnificent natural structure.

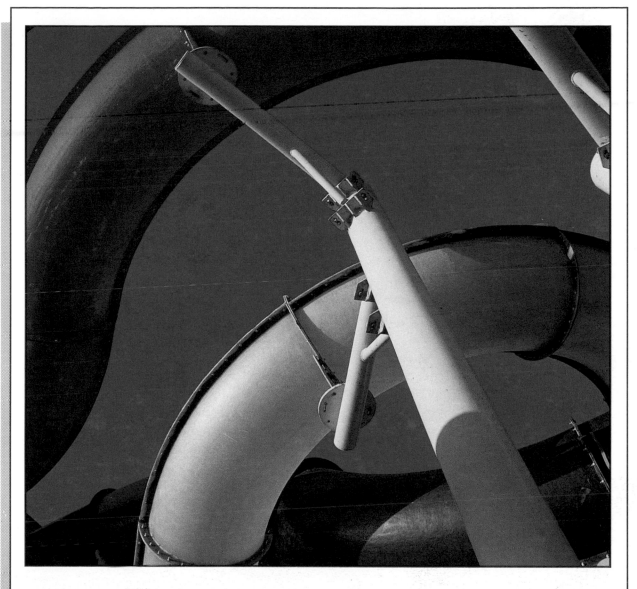

and think about the best materials to use before starting to build. New methods of building have been invented and new skills used. Designers and builders have learned from nature's structures and from scientific ideas about forces such as gravity and friction. New structures have been built by learning from the past and from the ideas of others. When a design fails the designer has to work out why before trying again.

We can observe the beauty and

This structure is part of a waterslide at a leisure centre.

strength of some of the world's great structures. We can find out more about nature's structures. We can see how houses, roads, skyscrapers, tunnels, bridges and other human-made structures have been built and have changed the way we live. We can build structures from our own designs and suggest how structures may look in the future.

Animals build structures

Many animals build structures which are complicated and beautiful. Spiders build webs of fine silk threads to catch their prey. The spider makes this silk in its body. Each web takes about an hour to make and a new one is made every day. If an insect touches the web it sticks to it and the spider catches it for food. Many kinds of spiders make webs. They are not all the same shape.

Birds build their nests in a variety of places and use different materials. Some nests are built in the branches of trees and hedges, while others are constructed on riverbanks or in tree trunks. Each kind of bird has a special way of making a nest. Grass and twigs might be used, and sometimes string will be woven in. Feathers or mud are often used to line the nest.

Sticklebacks are small fish that live in ponds and streams. The male stickleback builds a nest in which the female lays her eggs. First the male digs a channel in the bed of a stream. Into this he pushes small pieces of plants. This is bonded together with a sticky substance which he produces.

The beavers of Canada and the USA build spectacular dams. A beaver can fell a tree, gnaw off branches and float them along the river to where the dam is being built. It can carry gravel and mud in its forepaws to add to the dam structure. Having constructed a dam, a family of beavers build a dome-shaped lodge with underwater entrances, in which they will live.

A bullfinch feeds its young. Most birds make well constructed nests.

Watch a spider build its web

You need:

A small aquarium (or similar sized container)
Nylon netting
String
Damp soil

Shallow tray of water
Small plastic container with lid
Leafy twigs
Leafless twigs
Dead leaves and bark

1. Put a layer of damp soil in the bottom of the aquarium. Place a shallow tray of water on the soil. Add the leafy twigs, the dead leaves, the bark and the leafless twigs as shown. Cut the nylon netting so that it covers the top of the aquarium. Secure it with string. Always keep the cage damp. Keep it away from heat and direct sunlight.

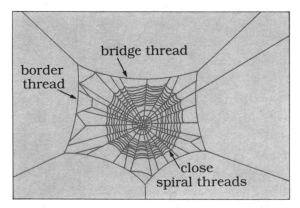

2. Now try to catch a garden spider. Find a damp place, for example inside a shed, in a greenhouse or under trees. Look for a web and then look for the spider. Catch it in your plastic container and put the lid on. Put it in your cage. Make sure the netting is tied on tightly.

3. Watch your spider while it builds its web. Make drawings to show the different stages.

4. Keep your spider for a few days then release it where you found it. If you keep it for more than a few days you will need to feed it on living flies.

The skeleton as a structure

Many animals have a skeleton and a backbone inside their bodies. These animals are called vertebrates. Humans are vertebrates and so are dogs, cats, fishes, birds and horses. The skeleton is an important structure which grows larger as the animal gets bigger.

There are more than 200 bones in your skeleton. Bones are hard and strong, but light in weight. They are different shapes and sizes. Your skeleton has three important tasks – it supports and protects the soft parts of your body and it helps you to move using muscles and joints. Your brain is protected by your skull, while your breastbone and ribs protect your heart and lungs. Your backbone is a long tube made up of many small bones called vertebrae. It protects your spinal cord. From your spinal cord, nerves run to all parts of your body.

Invertebrates are animals that do not have a backbone inside their bodies. Some invertebrates, such as earthworms and jellyfish, have no skeleton at all. Other invertebrates have an external skeleton which protects the animal. Lobsters, crabs and insects have external skeletons. Unfortunately, this skeleton does not grow with the animal. It has to be shed from time to time, leaving the animal unprotected while a new outer skeleton hardens.

When two bones meet in a skeleton structure they form a joint. Some joints, such as those in your arms and legs, help you to move around. You can swing your legs back and forwards and move your forearms. You can make these movements because your knees and elbows contain hinge joints. These joints move with the help of muscles. Most muscles work in pairs and are fixed to the bones of your skeleton by tendons.

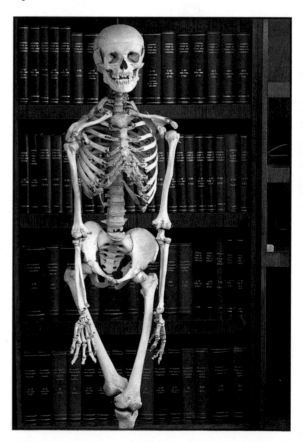

The human skeleton is a complex structure that supports the body.

Make a model arm

You need:
Stiff cardboard
Some paper fasteners
Glue
Elastic bands

1. Cut two lengths of cardboard, each measuring 20 cm by 5 cm. Use a paper fastener to hinge the two pieces together.

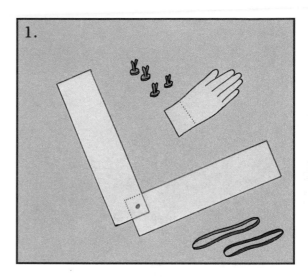

2. Glue a hand shape, made from cardboard, to the cardboard arm. Attach four more paper fasteners to the cards.

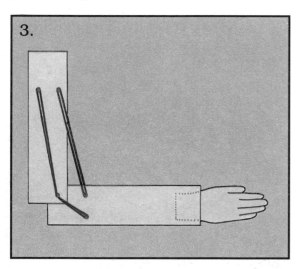

3. Fix two elastic bands to the paper fasteners. Move the forearm of your model to make the elbow joint bend. Notice how the top elastic shortens and the bottom elastic lengthens. Move the forearm down. What happens to the elastic?

Your arm moves in a similar way. Raise your forearm. Can you feel your biceps muscle? Use your triceps muscle to lower your forearm.

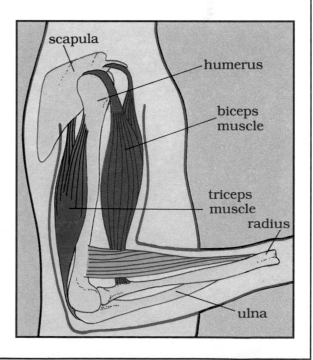

Trees

Trees are natural structures that we use to build houses and many other structures.

Trees have always played an important role in structures built by humans. Wood is needed for all kinds of buildings, from wigwams to modern-day houses. Trees are superb structures and are very important to life on Earth. Like other green plants, trees release the oxygen which we need to breathe and to live. When huge areas of forest are cut down, the homes and food sources of hundreds of animals are destroyed.

We can think of a tree as a superb machine with many parts. Each part has a special job to do. At the base of the tree are the spreading roots. The roots anchor the tree and stop it from blowing over in strong winds. The roots also absorb water and minerals from the soil. The trunk is rigid and supports the crown of the tree. The trunk is surrounded by bark which protects the tree.

Inside the trunk is the part we call wood. Here the water and minerals from the roots are carried, through tiny channels, up to the leaves. Food, made by the leaves, travels down the trunk to the roots in channels just under the bark. The crown of the tree is formed from leaves, twigs and branches. The leaves use the power of the sun to make energy for growth. They are arranged on the branches of a tree so that they catch as much sunlight as possible.

Study a tree

One of the best ways to appreciate the beauty of trees is to 'adopt' one. Choose a tree near your home or school. Use a reference book to identify your tree.

You need:
Camera and film
Paper and pencil
Wax crayons
Measuring tape

1. Make drawings and take photographs of the tree at various times of the year.

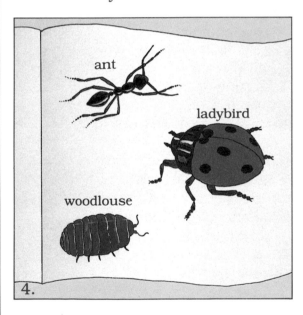

Visit your tree throughout a whole year to see how it changes. Keep a record of your findings in a notebook. Here are some ideas of things to do:

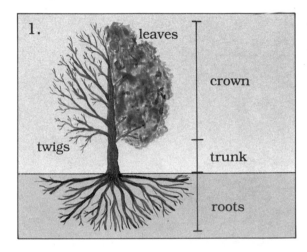

2. Make rubbings of the bark using a piece of paper and a wax crayon.

3. Measure the height and girth of the tree.

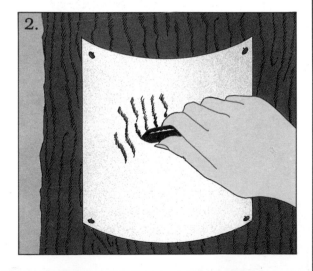

4. Find out which plants and animals live under and in the tree.

5. Find out how the timber of your tree might be used in making objects or structures.

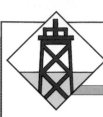

Super structures

The Sydney Opera House, in Australia, was opened in 1973. It took fifteen years to construct and is one of the most complicated structures ever built. The actual building site, at the entrance to Sydney Harbour, was small. Most of the building was made nearby and transported to the site. These pre-cast concrete parts were lifted into position by a crane.

The site for the Lloyd's Insurance Building in the centre of London was also small. But this building had to be designed to hold 6,000 workers.

The Sydney Opera House is one of Australia's biggest tourist attractions. It was designed to look like the sails of a ship.

To make more interior space the lifts and air-conditioning are built on to the outside of the building. The building has fourteen floors all focused around a massive, glass-covered central hall. This structure is covered by glass and steel and has a concrete and steel framework. It took nine years to build and cost £160 million.

When it was opened, in 1931, the Empire State Building, in the USA, was the tallest building in the world. It was erected in one of the busiest parts of New York with 102 floors. The foundations were excavated and the structure built without any interruption to the surrounding traffic. The building was constructed at a fantastic speed, taking less than two years from start to finish. Many people believed it would collapse, but it has even withstood a large aircraft crashing into the seventy-ninth floor. It stayed as the tallest building in the world until 1972.

The San Francisco-Oakland Bay Bridge has been described as one of the greatest human engineering achievements. The bridge withstood the force of the earthquake that occurred on 17 October 1989, which shows its strength. It is in fact two suspension bridges crossing a 3 km gap. The cables at the outer ends of the bridges are anchored on shore. But the ends of the cables are anchored to a massive human-made island. This remarkable island was constructed in the middle of the waterway using 31,000 tonnes of concrete.

The Empire State Building in New York, USA, was the world's highest building until 1972. It is still one of the world's most famous and impressive structures.

Materials

For thousands of years people used wood and stone to build structures. Local timber and stone was used because transporting materials from faraway places was expensive and difficult. The natural materials of an area are still used to build structures today. In countries with many forests, such as Canada and Norway, houses are often built of timber. In many countries local stone is quarried and used in buildings. But there are now a range of materials – bricks, concrete, steel, glass, timber – which can be used to build structures. We can build with these materials because we understand their properties and have developed skills in using them.

Many small buildings are built from bricks. Bricks are blocks of clay which have been baked hard in an oven. There are many different types of brick depending, mainly, on the type of clay used to make them. Timber is used to support floors, ceilings and roofs. It is also used for decorative purposes both inside and outside buildings.

It is only during the last century that we have learned how to build with steel and concrete. Today, structural steel is used in the form of girders or beams to build many large structures. The girders are fitted together, like a construction kit, and held in place with bolts. Concrete is a very important

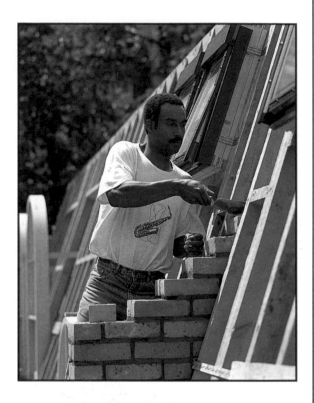

Here you can see several materials being used to build a house.

building material because it can do so many different jobs. Depending on the way it is mixed, it can be used for laying bricks, for waterproofing, and for laying floors and foundations. Engineers can make concrete even stronger by reinforcing it. Steel rods are placed inside the concrete before it hardens. Reinforced concrete is used in a variety of constructions. If the steel rod is stretched before the concrete hardens, then it is even stronger. This is called pre-stressed concrete.

Make a concrete beam

You need:
Cement
Sand
Very small stones or gravel
Bucket of water
70 cm length of wood (about 4 cm square)
Hardboard (30 cm x 12 cm)
Small trowel
Tin cans
Large old bowl
Newspaper
Petroleum jelly (Vaseline)
String
A sheet of polythene

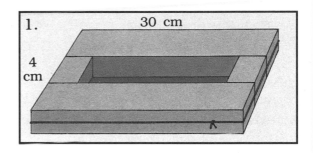

1. Cover your working surface with newspaper. Make a mould using some blocks of wood. Use a piece of hardboard or plywood as a base. Tie some string tightly around the mould. Lightly smear the inside of the mould with petroleum jelly.

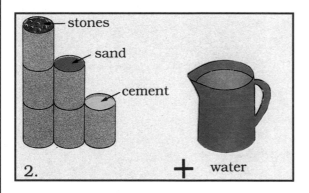

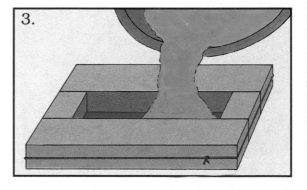

2. Make some concrete. Wear gloves to protect your hands and ask an adult to help you. Use a large tin can as a measure. Measure out one can of cement powder, three cans of small stones, and two cans of sand. Mix these materials together in a bowl and stir in a little water. Use the trowel or a piece of wood to mix the materials. The mixture should be quite stiff. Wash your hands after making concrete.

3. Pour your concrete into the mould. Use a piece of wood to tap the concrete to push out any air bubbles. Cover your concrete with a piece of polythene and leave it to harden overnight. It will harden best in damp and cool surroundings.

4. Can you design an experiment to test the strength of your concrete? Could you make a reinforced concrete beam?

Foundations

In planning structures engineers know, from past experience, that they must lay firm foundations. The Leaning Tower of Pisa, in Italy, is one example of what happens when the foundations are inadequate. All structures press down on the earth on which they are built. The walls of houses are built on a concrete base.

This base is wider than the walls so that the weight of the house is spread over a larger area. With massive structures, such as skyscrapers, the pressure on the earth is very great and special foundations must be laid.

The earth on which the structure is to be built is carefully examined. Samples of soil and rock are studied before engineers decide on the type of foundations to lay. Sometimes a building which is tall and heavy, but which has a small base, is built on a flat slab of concrete. Thousands of tonnes of concrete are used to build these 'raft' foundations.

On very soft soils the foundations may be formed from vast concrete boxes. The space in the boxes may be used for storage and car-parking. At other times structures are built on rods or piles which are driven deep into the earth. These piles are made of concrete and steel. The machines which drive these piles into the ground have to be very powerful. Often a huge raft of concrete joins the piles together and the structure is built on top of this solid base.

The most important parts of a building are its foundations. They must be strong enough to support the weight of the finished structure. These are the foundations for a hotel in Turkey.

Laying foundations

You need:

5 large tin cans of equal size (empty and clean)
Cement powder
Sand
Very small stones or gravel

Bucket of water
Small trowel
Piece of wood
An old bowl
Can opener
A sheet of polythene

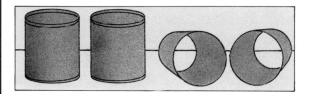

1. Use the can opener to remove the top and bottom sections from four of the tin cans. You should be left with four tin can cylinders as shown.

2. Find a spot in your garden where the soil is quite soft. Make a square shape by pushing the tin cans into the soil so that the rims are just level with the surface, with the cylinders about 10 cm apart.

3. Make some concrete. Wear gloves to protect your hands and ask an adult to help you. Use the fifth tin can as a measure. Measure out one can of cement powder, three cans of small stones, and two cans of sand. Mix these materials together in an old bowl and stir in some water. Do not use too much water. Use the trowel or a piece of wood to mix the materials. The mixture should be quite stiff.

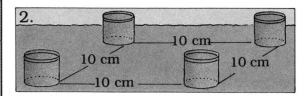

4. Pour your concrete into the four tin cylinders fixed in the ground. Use a piece of wood to tap the concrete to push out any air bubbles. Cover your concrete with a sheet of polythene and leave to harden overnight. Wash your hands after using concrete.

5. You have now made the pile foundations for a small structure. How could you make a small concrete 'raft' to fit on top of these piles? What could you use as a mould for the concrete?

Houses and roads

The people of the world make their houses using many different materials. In some hot, dry countries mud is mixed with straw to build small round huts. Some people live on houseboats, while others live in timber houses built on stilts in rivers. Important factors in the design of homes are the climate and the materials available to build the houses.

Many houses have brick walls. To keep the house warm the walls are built in two layers with an air-gap in between. This cavity between the outer and inner walls is often filled with an insulating material to prevent heat escaping. To build the roof a framework of wood is constructed. This is finished with roofing felt and tiles.

We rely very much on motor transport in our everyday lives.

People travel on roads to get to work or school, visit friends or just to have a day out. Many goods are transported by road. New roads are being built in all parts of the world. Engineers have to decide how to build them and which materials to use. Many modern roads are built to allow vehicles to travel at high speeds over long distances. In Britain these roads are called motorways. In North America they are known as freeways or expressways. Large earth-moving machines are used to prepare the ground for a new road. Firm foundations are needed and often reinforced concrete is laid. The top surface of a road is made of concrete or asphalt.

Large cities, such as Los Angeles, USA, have complex road systems.

Design a house

You need:
Cardboard boxes
Plastic trays
Construction kits (with building blocks)
Wood structures materials
(see page 22)
Scissors
Pencil, ruler, paper
Brushes and paints

Design and build a model of your ideal house. First you will need to think carefully about questions like these:

Will your house have one floor or more?
What sort of materials will you use to construct the outside of the house?
How many doors will it have?
How many windows will your ideal house have?
Will the roof be flat or sloping?
How many rooms will the house have?
Will the rooms be large or small?
Where will the house be built?

Ask an adult to take you to a building site so that you can get more ideas. Draw sketches of your plans. Use the building blocks from a construction kit to help in building your model house. Use materials you can find around home or at school to help you.

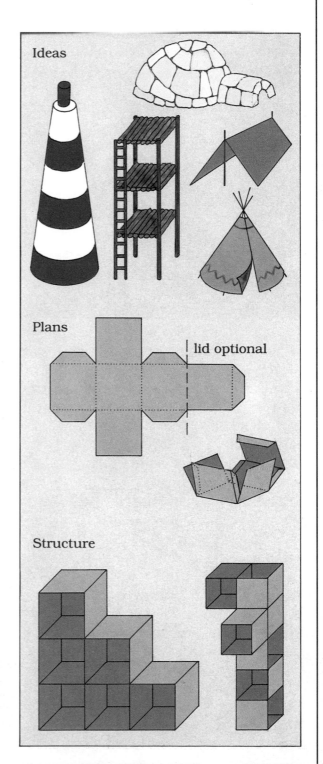

Ideas

Plans

lid optional

Structure

Skyscrapers

Ontario in Canada has many skyscrapers.

In many cities there is a great shortage of room for office buildings. One solution is to make the buildings taller. Building such high structures poses a number of problems. The buildings are very heavy, creating great pressure on the foundations and on the lower parts of the building. Such tall structures are exposed to the wind which can cause damage both to the top of the skyscraper and to the base. They need to be able to stand the pushes and pulls of hurricanes. Fire is another great risk in skyscrapers. How can people escape and how can the fire be extinguished?

As more and more skyscrapers are built, engineers have become better at dealing with the problems. The Manhattan area of New York, USA, where there are many skyscrapers, has hard rock foundations. This means less work is needed to prepare the ground for building than if clay was present. The engineers build massive frameworks using steel and concrete. Powerful cranes are used to lift steel girders into position. These frameworks are built to withstand more forces than they will ever have to endure.

Skyscrapers can sway in the wind. To counteract this, huge weights are positioned on rollers on top of the building. As the skyscraper moves with the wind, so the weights move too, taming the swaying. Fire-fighting systems come on automatically once a fire is detected on any floor of a skyscraper.

Building towers

You need:

Newspapers
Sticky tape
Drinking straws
Small plastic container
Water
Pipe cleaners
Card (each sheet measuring 29 cm
x 21 cm)
Scissors

You can have fun building frameworks. Here are some challenges to try with your friends.

1.

Challenge 1

Who can build the tallest tower, using a newspaper and some sticky tape? You have thirty minutes to complete this challenge.

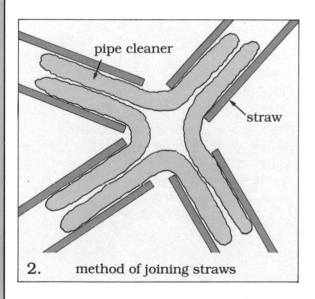

pipe cleaner

straw

2. method of joining straws

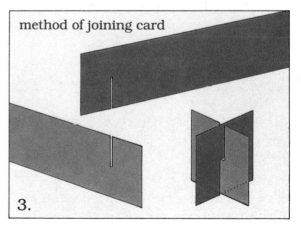

method of joining card

3.

Challenge 2

Use some drinking straws to build a framework as high as you can. Use pipe cleaners to join the straws together. The diagram above will show you how to begin your framework.

Challenge 3

Who can build a tower, using only one sheet of card, which will support a small plastic container of water? You can use scissors to cut the card but no other materials are to be used.

Building wood structures

You need:
Some lengths of 1 cm square wood
A small hacksaw
A bench hook
Some thin card
PVA glue
Ruler, pencil and scissors

1. Use your ruler and pencil to draw horizontal lines at 3 cm intervals on a sheet of card. Draw vertical lines at 3 cm intervals. Now draw diagonal lines as shown.

2. Cut out as many right-angled triangles as you need.

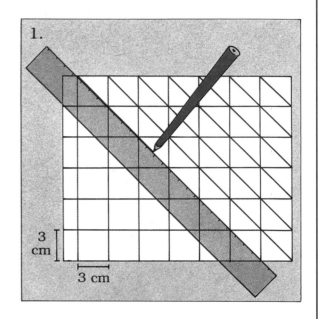

1.

3 cm

3 cm

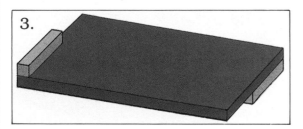

3.

3. Make a bench hook. Take a piece of wood about 15 cm long, 10 cm wide and 1 or 2 cms thick. Fix (nail or glue) two strips of wood, each measuring about 6 cm long and 1 cm square, to both sides of the piece of wood.

4. Mark out 40 cm on a length of 1 cm square wood. Use the hacksaw and bench hook to saw through the wood. Place the bench hook on the edge of a table. Hold the wood on top of the bench hook as shown. Use the hacksaw to cut through the wood on top of the bench hook. Ask an adult to help you.

5. Repeat this so that you have four lengths of wood measuring 40 cm, and eight lengths of wood measuring 10 cm each.

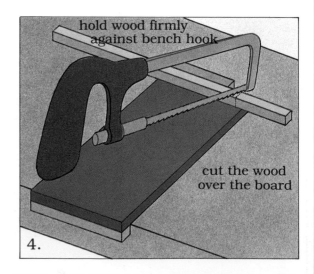

hold wood firmly against bench hook

cut the wood over the board

4.

6. Take two 10 cm lengths of wood and place them at right angles to each other. Apply some PVA glue to one side of a card triangle and position it over the corner. Let it dry. Repeat this process so that you have a rectangle measuring 10 cm by 12 cm. Carefully turn this rectangle over and glue further triangles to each corner. Let the frame set.

7. Make a further rectangle exactly the same size as the one above. Use 8 card triangles, as before, to make the joints.

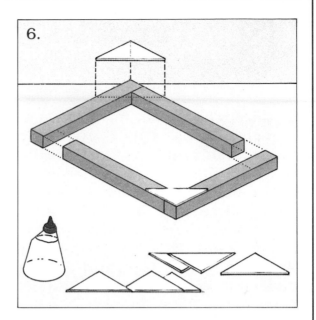

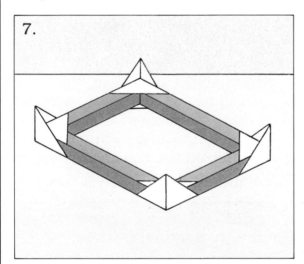

8. Take two triangles and glue them, as shown, to one corner of one of your rectangles. Glue triangles to each of the other corners. Allow them all to set. Repeat this with the second rectangle.

9. Glue the four 40 cm uprights into position. Allow the joints to set.

You have now made a simple box structure. You can use this method to make a number of structures such as houses, skyscrapers, lighthouses, oil rigs, cranes (see page 41), windmills and bridges. Make some wood structures of your own design. Remember to draw your design carefully before you begin constructing.

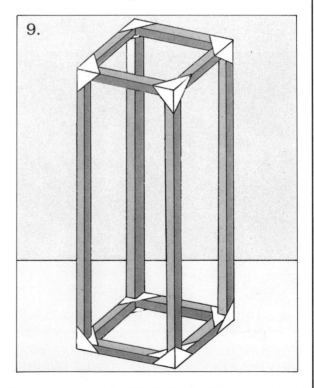

Tunnels

Engineers have built many kinds of tunnels so that cars, lorries and trains can travel under cities, beneath rivers and through mountains. Large-scale tunnelling only became possible after explosives were developed. One hundred and fifty years ago the great British engineer Isambard Brunel built the first underwater tunnel beneath the River Thames.

Before constructing a tunnel, testing takes place to see if the ground is suitable for tunnelling. If the ground is hard then explosives are used to blast it away. Powerful drills, driven by compressed air, are used to bore into rock. The Mont Blanc Tunnel between Italy and France is 11 km long and was blasted through solid rock.

When the ground is soft a steel tunnelling shield is used. This stops the tunnel from collapsing as it is being dug. The shield is forced forwards into the ground and the earth removed from inside the shield by powerful machines. The tunnel is lined with steel or concrete as the shield moves forward.

Another way of making tunnels is to use ready-built sections. This method is used to cross a river where the ground is extremely soft. Dredgers dig a trench in the river bed. Steel tunnel tubes are made on land and then floated into position and sunk into the trench. Concrete is laid around the steel tube to hold it in place on the river bed.

A tunnel being dug through a hillside in Switzerland.

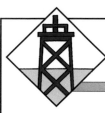

Testing tunnel shapes

You need:
Some thin cardboard
Sticky tape
Some metal washers

Look at the tunnel in the photograph. Why is it this shape? Are all tunnels this shape? Cut five rectangular pieces of card of equal size. Make some tunnel shapes as suggested below. Use sticky tape to hold your shapes in place.

V-shaped tunnel

Triangular-shaped tunnel

Rectangular-shaped tunnel

Tube-shaped tunnel

Horse-shoe shaped tunnel

Which shape will carry the most weight? Use the metal washers to test them. What other things does an engineer have to think about when designing a tunnel?

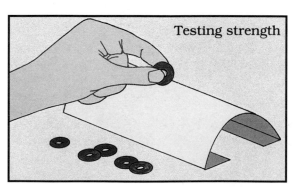
Testing strength

Tunnel shapes

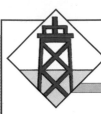

The Channel Tunnel

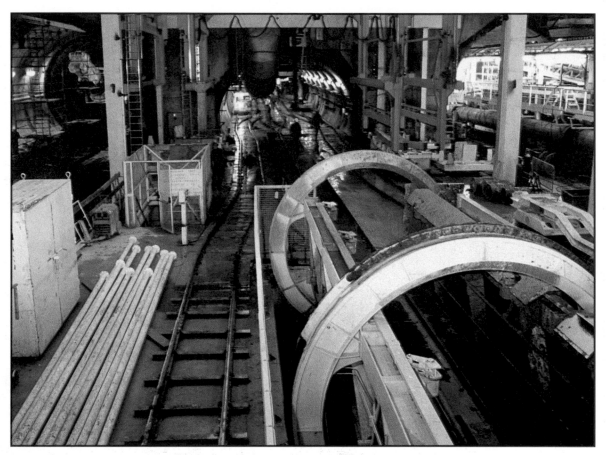

This is the entrance to the Channel Tunnel in Sangatte, France.

The Channel Tunnel, which is due to open in 1993, will be the first tunnel link between Britain and France. The construction of this tunnel, which is 50 km long, is the biggest engineering project ever undertaken in Europe. Fifteen thousand workers are using advanced machinery to build this structure with 38 km of tunnel actually passing under the English Channel. It is, in fact, made up of three separate tunnels. All three tunnels will run parallel to each other and they will have smaller connecting tunnels at intervals. High-speed trains will use the two larger tunnels. The third tunnel will be a service tunnel. It will be used for maintenance work and ventilation.

The engineers have to work in dangerous, hot and wet conditions. Using special giant boring machines, they have to tunnel through chalk filled with water. They are at work on both sides of the Channel and will meet in the middle. The latest technology, including laser beam guidance, is being used to make sure the tunnel is following the correct course.

Millions of people will use the tunnel when it is open. Many will travel on fully-automatic rail shuttles. Cars, lorries and coaches will board these shuttles and travel at 160 kph through the tunnel. Many other travellers will use high-speed trains (HSTs) which will be designed to travel from London to Paris in three hours. The tunnel designers have had to consider the possibility of train accidents and fires within the tunnel. The service tunnel will be used in emergencies to evacuate passengers.

A section of the Channel Tunnel under construction, showing part of the railway track. The 50-km long tunnel is scheduled to open in 1993.

Bridges

A clapper bridge in Devon, England. This very early bridge design involves laying slabs of stone across other stones.

Bridges are structures which allow us to cross rivers, valleys, railway lines and roads. The earliest bridges were probably trees which had fallen across streams. People would use these when they were moving from place to place. Some early bridges were made of stone slabs laid across other stones. They were called clapper bridges.

Before building a bridge the engineers have to work out answers to many questions. How long will the bridge need to be? How high should it be? Where will the foundations be built? How much traffic will it have to carry? What materials should be used? How much will it cost? Can it be made to look attractive? Does anything have to pass underneath the bridge? Every part of the bridge will be planned out on paper before the building starts.

If the distance to be bridged is short then the engineers will build a beam bridge. It may consist of a long piece of steel or wood supported at each end by piers. A way of increasing the span of the bridge is to use a framework of trusses. If the bridge is crossing a shallow river then a number of piers may be built to support the beam. Beam bridges are very common on motorways. Like many modern bridges these motorway bridges are built using concrete and steel.

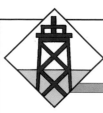

Build a beam bridge

You need:
Newspaper
Cardboard
Polystyrene
Sticky tape
Glue
String

The problem:
Can you design and build a beam bridge to span a distance of 50 cm? Try to build a bridge which is strong enough to hold a brick.

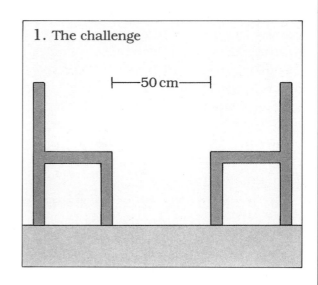

1. The challenge

|←—50 cm—→|

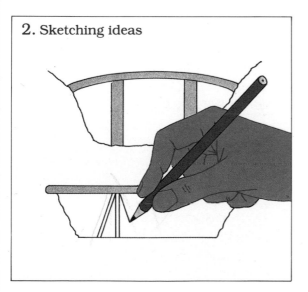

2. Sketching ideas

3. Testing your idea

Collect ideas:
You may find it useful to go to the library and look at books about bridge construction.

Make drawings:
As ideas come to mind, sketch your solutions to the problem.

Select your best idea:
Think carefully about your ideas. Which one will work best? Make a careful drawing of your best idea. Construct your best idea, and test it. Does it solve the problem? Make some changes so that the bridge is even stronger.

Arch and cantilever bridges

Arch bridges can span greater distances than simple beam bridges. The Romans built many arch bridges of wood and stone. Some of these are still standing. The An-Chi Bridge was built by the Chinese around the year 600. This 36 m bridge is one of the oldest arch bridges in the world and it is still in use today.

An arch bridge gets its strength from the force exerted sideways, against its ends, or abutments. The bricks or stones which form the arch are wedge-shaped. The keystone in the centre of the arch is often larger than the other stones. The abutments have to be well-built. Modern arch bridges are built of steel and are able to carry cars and trains. The Sydney Harbour Bridge spans 503 m across Australia's busiest harbour. The railway tracks and roadways are suspended from the arch.

The Forth Railway Bridge in Scotland is a very large cantilever bridge. It spans 2,529 m and is constructed from steel. Each unit of the bridge is made up of a pier which supports a cantilever arm on each side. Sometimes these arms are connected directly to other cantilever arms. The cantilever arms of the Forth Railway Bridge are connected by suspended girder sections.

The Forth Railway Bridge in Scotland is a cantilever bridge.

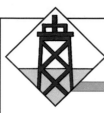

Build a cantilever bridge

You need:
Some paper fasteners
50 strips of card (each measuring
8 cm by 2 cm)
A hole punch
A strong cardboard box

The cantilever arms of a cantilever bridge stick out from the pier. Can you build a cantilever arm which sticks out from the side of a cardboard box?

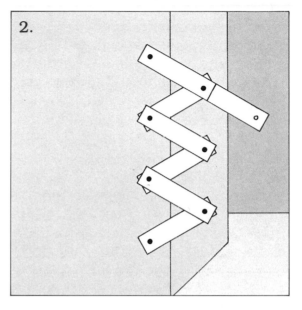

2.

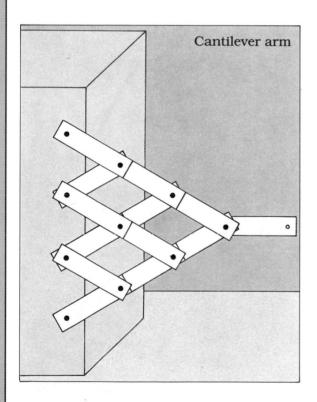

Cantilever arm

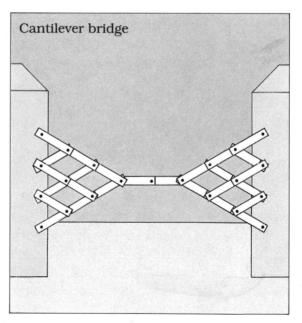

Cantilever bridge

1. Begin by punching holes in each end of the card strips. You can join the strips together using the paper fasteners.

2. Fix some strips to the side of the box using the paper fasteners. How far can you build outwards using the card strips?

Suspension bridges

Modern suspension bridges can span much greater distances than other bridges. Suspension bridges look very graceful but are immensely strong. The roadway hangs from cables carried by two towers.

After years of planning the engineers construct the foundations for the massive twin towers. Careful investigations are needed to find out the best types of foundations to build. Sometimes underwater work chambers, or caissons, need to be constructed, so that the engineers can work on the foundations in deep water. Once the foundations are ready the steel towers are constructed. The great suspension bridges have towers which are as high as a 70-storey skyscraper and are built over a kilometre apart.

When the towers are completed, the laying of the cables begins. The cables have to be strong enough to support the roadway and to withstand extreme weather conditions. The cables are fixed to huge anchorages at each end of the bridge. These structures are made of reinforced concrete and are able to stand the continuous pull of the cables and roadway. If either anchorage failed then the bridge would collapse.

The roadway is added when the towers, cables and anchorages are completed. Sections of the roadway are hoisted into position and suspended from steel ropes. The weight of the complete roadway will make the cables sag. The amount of sag will already have been calculated by the bridge designers.

The Verrazano-Narrows Bridge (New York), the Golden Gate Bridge (San Francisco), the Forth Road Bridge (Edinburgh), and the Humber Bridge (Hull) are amongst the great suspension bridges of the world.

The Golden Gate Bridge in San Francisco, USA, is one of the world's best-known suspension bridges.

A model suspension bridge

You need:

Two identical cardboard boxes (such as tissue boxes or cereal cartons)
A baseboard of stiff cardboard
Some thick card
Scissors
Glue
Sticky tape
Some thick string
Thread
Paper fasteners

1. Cut an identical rectangular section from each box as shown.

2. Glue the cardboard boxes to the baseboard. They should be about 60 cm apart and be parallel to each other.

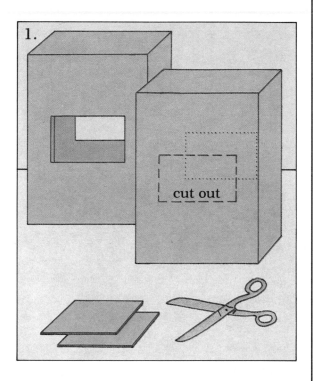

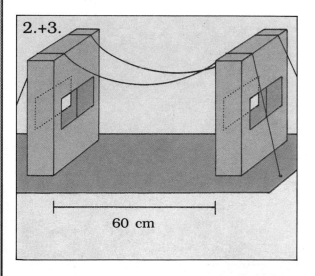

3. Run two pieces of thick string over each box and fasten the ends to the baseboard using paper fasteners.

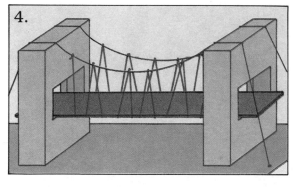

4. Cut a piece of thick card to form the roadway. Fix it in place through the towers. Use some thread to hang the roadway from the thick string.

Can you design a better model suspension bridge? Draw your design before you start making it.

Islands in the sea

Seventy per cent of the Earth's surface is covered by water. Hidden beneath the oceans is a vast undersea world. Scientists and engineers have begun to explore this hostile environment to use its wealth for the benefit of humankind.

Oil is an important part of the modern world, providing most of our energy. As we use more and more oil so the search for new oilfields has spread under the sea. To start with, the oil was extracted from shallow waters but now drilling takes place in deep water all around the world.

The search for oil below the sea has meant that special drilling rigs have had to be designed and built. These drilling rigs have been fitted on structures which can float on the water, and yet be capable of withstanding stormy seas and very high winds. In shallow waters jack-up rigs are used. The legs can be attached to the sea-bed and the platform jacked-up to the required height above the sea. Another type – the semi-submersible drilling rig – floats on huge buoyancy chambers located below the surface of the sea. Heavy anchors keep the rig in position.

Oil rigs at sea are designed to withstand strong currents and huge waves.

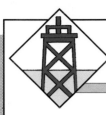

Make a paper tower

You need:
Some sheets of newspaper
Sticky tape
Scissors
A pot of marbles

1. Roll a sheet of newspaper into a tube. Stick the edges with the tape. Is your paper strong enough to support the pot of marbles?

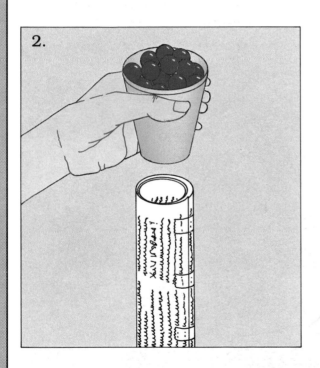

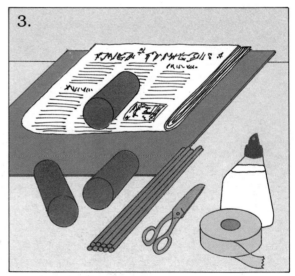

2. Test it. Lower the pot slowly on to the tower. Watch what happens. How could you make your tower stronger? Look at photographs of drilling rigs and production platforms. Have you noticed how tubes are used to construct them? Why do you think this is?

3. Design and make a model drilling rig or production platform. Use materials such as cardboard tubes, newspapers, straws, thick and thin cardboard, sticky tape, glue, scissors. Your structure must be well designed and constructed. Could you test it in the wind?

Building dams

In some countries the height of the river water changes with the seasons of the year. Sometimes there will be a danger of floods, while at other times the rivers dry up. To help control the flow of water engineers build dams. These giant structures are used to prevent floods, to supply water to homes, to supply water for growing crops and to provide hydroelectric power.

Before starting to build the dam the course of the river must be temporarily changed. A new channel or tunnel may be built to divert the river. The engineers have to decide which materials to use in building the dam. Some dams are built from rock and earth. This may be cheaper

A dam in a beautiful valley in the Dolomites, Italy. The wall of the dam must be immensely strong to retain the water behind it.

if these materials are available near the site of the dam. Other dams are constructed from millions of tonnes of reinforced concrete. Rock and earth dams need to be much thicker than concrete dams. Both types of dam are broader at the base than at the top. This is because the deepest part of the dam has the greatest pressure of water on it.

Dams are expensive and take a long time to build. But they bring great benefits to the communities where they are constructed.

Investigating water pressure

You need:
Large tin can
Hammer and nail
Jug of water
Sticky tape

1. Use the hammer and nail to make a row of six holes in the side of the empty tin can. The holes should be the same distance apart. Cover the holes with a strip of sticky-tape.

2. Take the can outside and fill it with water. Pull away the strip of sticky tape.

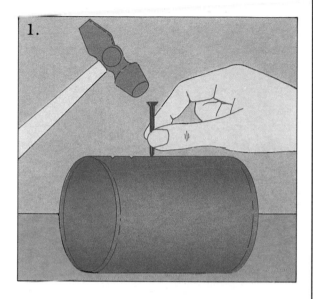

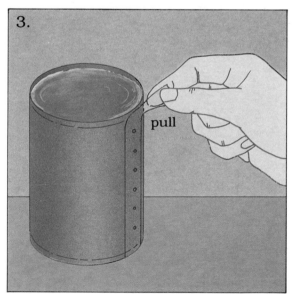

pull

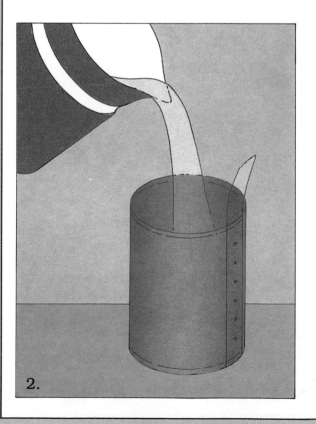

3. Watch how the water escapes through the holes. Where is the water flow the weakest? Where is the water flow the strongest? Does this explain why dams are built to be stronger at the base than at the top?

The Thames Barrier

In recent years experts have feared that a high tide combined with strong winds would cause water to surge up the River Thames and flood large areas of London, England. They decided to build a massive steel barrier across the river to prevent such a disaster.

Huge steel gates are positioned between nine concrete piers which have been built across the river. These gates usually lie flat on the river bed so that ships can pass up and down the river. When there is a danger of floods the gates are raised to form a continuous steel barrier across the river. The barrier is under the water most of the time, so engineers had to ensure that the structure was designed to withstand the force of the river. It also had to be built from materials that would not corrode.

The Thames Barrier protects the city of London from floods.

River barrages

The world population is increasing all the time and we are using more energy than ever before. At the moment most of our energy comes from fossil fuels such as coal, oil and natural gas. Fossil fuels, however, cannot last for ever. Engineers are therefore searching for new sources of energy. One possibility is to use the force of the tides.

To harness tidal energy, engineers need to build massive concrete and steel structures, called barrages, across rivers affected by tides. The

The River Rance barrier in France is a tidal energy scheme.

rising and falling tide turns turbines which make electricity. A barrage can produce the same amount of electricity as a large power station.

At present there are only two tidal energy schemes in use in the world. One is near St Malo in France and the other is in Nova Scotia, Canada. There are plans to build barrages in Britain, on the River Severn and on the River Mersey.

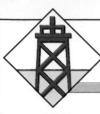

Cranes

Cranes are essential for building large structures when heavy objects have to be lifted.

Cranes are used in building structures to lift heavy objects such as steel girders. A simple crane has a movable arm or jib from which hangs a cable with a hook or bucket attached to it. The cable runs on a pulley at the end of the jib and is attached to a winch. The load on the hook or in the bucket can be raised or lowered by winding in or paying out the cable. The load can be moved horizontally by moving the jib.

There are a number of different types of cranes. On building sites the tower crane is now a familiar sight. It has a horizontal jib with a heavy concrete counterweight at one end. The crane is constructed from a framework of thin steel girders. Sometimes tower cranes are erected inside skyscrapers and are dismantled when the building is almost completed.

Cranes are essential for the building of structures but are also used to demolish them. Have you seen a crane swinging a heavy metal ball to demolish a building?

Build a model crane

You need:
Some lengths of 1 cm square wood
A small hacksaw
A bench hook
Cotton reels
Dowel rods
Thick card
Thin card

1. Follow the instructions on pages 22–3 to make a box structure to use as a tower crane.

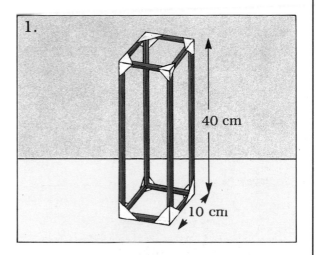

1.

40 cm

10 cm

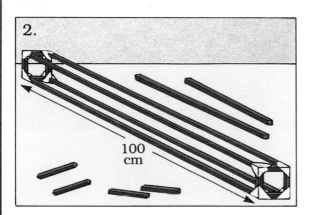

2.

100 cm

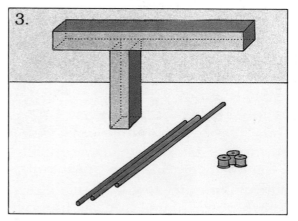

3.

2. Make the horizontal jib. Cut four lengths of wood measuring 100 cm each. Cut eight lengths of wood each measuring 10 cm. Cut some card triangles. Make a box structure as shown. Cut some more lengths of wood and add them to your framework to give added strength.

3. Fit the jib on top of the tower you have already made. You may need to make the tower more rigid by adding further wood pieces.

Some challenges for you:
How can you make the jib move horizontally from side to side? The dowel rod, cotton reels and card may help.

Can you make a pulley arrangement so that your crane can pick up a load?

How stable is your crane?

How can you stop it tipping over?

Structures for the future

Over the past hundred years people have built many new structures in an effort to shape and improve the environment in which we live. New materials have been developed and used. Complex machines have been invented for construction work. Many problems have been encountered and solved.

How will the structures of the future look? Will skyscrapers get taller? Will tunnels and bridges get longer? Will different types of dams be built? Will people want to live in cities or will they choose to live closer to nature? Nobody knows the answers to these questions. We do know that our world is faced with a number of great problems. One is that the population of many countries is rising very quickly, causing overcrowding and traffic congestion in towns and cities. Another problem is that the fuels we depend on, such as oil and gas, are gradually running out. We will need to save fuel and develop other ways to make energy.

It may be that we will make more use of the energy coming directly from the sun and the wind. Perhaps more people will live in houses built underground or live on structures built on the sea. Will more structures be built below the seas? Will we build in space? Will people live and work in space colonies? New materials will be developed and used

A 33-m high wind turbine in New Mexico, USA.

in the buildings of the future. Computers will be used even more than now to design, to build and in the day-to-day running of many of these structures.

A structure of the future

You need:
Cardboard boxes
Plastic bottles
Cardboard tubes
Empty drinks cans
Yoghurt pots
Glue, sticky tape
Scissors
Paints and brushes
Wood structures materials (see pages 22 and 46)

Design and make
Can you design and make a structure that might be built in the future? Here are some ideas to choose from:

1. A human-made island to be towed out to sea.
2. A structure to be built in space.

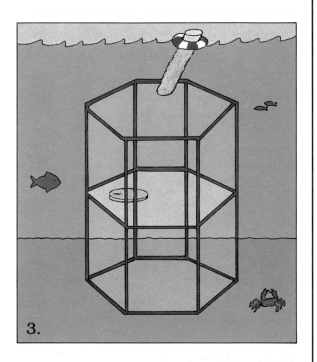

3.

1.

3. A structure to be built underwater.
4. A small town to be built on another planet.
5. A skyscraper.

4.

You will need to think of the problems of living and working in these places. Look in books to find out more. Sketch some designs. Build a model from one of your designs. Use any materials you can find around your home or school.

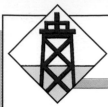

Glossary

Asphalt A black, tarlike material used on road surfaces.

Beam The horizontal part of a framework.

Cantilever A beam, girder or framework that is fixed at one end only.

Cement A powder of limestone and clay. When mixed with water it sets into a hard mass.

Colonies Communities of people who live far away from their original homeland.

Concrete A modern building material which is made of small stones, cement and sand. When mixed with water it makes a stiff paste which sets hard. When steel rods are added it is very strong and is called reinforced concrete.

Corrode To be eaten away by the action of chemicals, moisture or air as in the rusting of metal.

Crane A machine used for lifting and moving large weights.

Foundations The lowest part of a structure which takes the structure's weight.

Friction Resistance to motion when two surfaces are in contact.

Girder A long beam made of steel or concrete.

Gravity The force with which the Earth attracts an object.

Invertebrates Animals which do not have a backbone.

Jib The lifting arm of a crane.

Pile A pillar of concrete or steel driven into the ground to support a weight.

Properties Qualities or characteristics of a material such as density or strength.

Shuttles Buses, trains or aircraft that travel back and forth between two points.

Span The distance between the supports of a bridge.

Truss A rigid framework.

Ventilation Providing clean air.

Vertebrates Animals with a backbone and skeleton.

Winch A machine used for raising or lowering weights.

Books to read

Dixon, M, *Young Engineer on the Road* (Wayland, 1983)
Dixon, M, *Young Engineer on the Waterway* (Wayland, 1983)
Lambert, M, *Focus on Building Materials* (Wayland, 1988)
Lambert, M, *Homes in the Future* (Wayland, 1988)
Rickard, G, *Building Homes* (Wayland, 1988)
Whitlock, R, *Exploring Buildings* (Wayland, 1987)

Further information

Places to visit

Australia

Museum of Victoria
328 Swanston Street
Melbourne
Victoria 3000

Powerhouse Museum
500 Harris Street
Ultimo
NSW 2007

Snowy Mountains Hydroelectric
  Commission
Yarrang Street
Monaro Highway
Cooma
NSW 2630

Britain

Avoncroft Museum of Buildings
Stoke Heath
Bromsgrove
Worcestershire

Beamish Open Air Museum
Stanley
Nr. Sunderland
Tyne and Wear

The Building Innovation Gallery
The Building Centre
113–115 Portland Street
Manchester M1 6FB

Ironbridge Gorge Museum
Ironbridge
Telford
Shropshire

Landmark (Highland Heritage Park)
Carrbridge
Near Aviemore
Inverness-shire

Thames Barrier Visitors' Centre
Unity Way
Woolwich
London SE18 5NJ

Young Designers' Centre
London Design Centre
Haymarket
London SW1

New Zealand

Auckland Building Exhibition
  Centre
PO Box 271
Auckland 1

Try to visit:

Skyscrapers, tunnels, bridges and other structures near your home. Ask an adult to take you to a building site. When on holiday try to visit some of the 'famous structures' of the world.

Organizations to contact

Australia

BHP Co Ltd (for steel)
140 William Street
Melbourne
Victoria 3000

Cement and Concrete Association
  of Australia
60 Albert Road
South Melbourne
Victoria 3208

Pilkington (Australia) Ltd (for glass)
Product Information Centre
7th Floor
420 St Kilda Road
Melbourne
Victoria 3004

Timber Development Centre
525 Elizabeth Street
Sydney
NSW 2000

Britain

British Steel Corporation
Information Services
9 Albert Embankment
London SE1

Cement and Concrete Association
Wrexham Springs
Slough
SL3 6PL

National Federation of Clay
  Industries
Drayton House
30 Gordon Street
London WC1

Timber Research and Development
  Association
Hughenden Valley
High Wycombe
Bucks
HP14 4ND

Canada

Try to contact your local Visitors
and Convention Bureau for
information about your area.

Canada's Capital Visitors and
  Convention Bureau
222 Queen Streeet
7th Floor
Ottawa
Ontario K1P 5V9

Department of Development
PO Box 2016
Yellowknife
NWT X1A 2C5

Northern Frontier Visitors
  Association
Box 1107
Yellow knife
NWT X1A 2C5

New Zealand

Building Research Association of
  New Zealand
PO Box 17–214
Greenland
Auckland 5

Institute of Professional Engineers
PO Box 6748
Auckland 1

Ministry of Forestry
PO Box 39
Auckland 1

New Zealand Concrete Research
  Association
Private bag
Porirua
Wellington

New Zealand Timber Industry
PO Box 308
Wellington

Remember to send a stamped
addressed envelope with your
enquiry.

Notes for parents and teachers

Teachers will find this book useful in implementing the National Curriculum at Key Stages 1, 2 and 3. Within *Structures* there is information and activities relating to:

Technology – Attainment Targets 1, 2, 3 and 4
Science – Attainment Targets 1, 2, 5, 6, 7, 8, 9, 10 and 11

Structures can be developed as a cross-curricular topic involving English and Mathematics.

There are many activities in this book which will require the help of a teacher or parent. Parents will also find the section on places to visit helpful during weekends and school holidays.

Picture Acknowledgements

The photographs in this book were provided by:
Bruce Coleman: Fritz Prenzel 4, 12, Norman Tomalin 20, 32, John Topham 42; Eye Ubiquitous 5, 30, 38, 40; Hutchison 6, 16, 18, 28; Topham 26, 27; Wayland 10, 34; Zefa *cover* (F. Damm), 8, 13, 14, 24, 36, 39. All illustrations by Jenny Hughes.

Index